P9-BIK-134

VIETNAM

OPENING DOORS TO THE WORLD

DEDICATION

This book is dedicated to the many thousands of American men and women who went off to Vietnam because they believed it was their duty. The country they returned to did not always welcome them as heroes, and all too often they did not receive the dignity they deserved. Regardless of whether the readers of this book believe the Vietnam war was wrong or right, the Americans who fell there and those who came home deserve to be honored for doing what was asked of them in the most confusing of times.

Library of Congress Cataloging-in-Publication Data

Graetz, Rick
  Vietnam, opening doors to the world.
  world.
  1. Vietnam--Description and travel--
     1975--Guide- books
  2. Vietnam--Description and travel--
     1975--Views.
     I. Rohrbach, Fred. II. Title
  DS 556.39, G73 1988
  915.97' 0444 88-7479
  ISBN 0-938314-57-2(pbk.)

ISBN 0-938314-57-2

© 1988 American
Geographic Publishing,
Helena, Montana

All rights reserved

William A. Cordingley,
  Chairman

Rick Graetz,
  Publisher

MarkThompson,
  Director of Publications

Barbara Fifer,
  Production Manager

Design by Len Visual

Printed in Korea
  by Dong-A Printing Co.

Front Cover Photo: Ha Long Bay north of Haiphong.

Back Cover Photos: Central market of Ho Chi Minh City.
Woman in the village of Mo Buc.
Village elder in Bao Loc.
Rice harvest in the Mekong Delta.

Preceding Page: The Perfume River and The Citadel at Hue.

Facing Page: Citizen of Hanoi.

VIETNAM

OPENING DOORS TO THE WORLD

by Rick Graetz
Assisted by Fred Rohrbach
Foreword by Stanley Karnow
Photography by Rick Graetz unless otherwise credited

American Geographic Publishing

Putting together travel arrangements for an extensive trip to a country such as Vietnam is not easy. And to include in the plans work on a book about a country that has heretofore been closed to westerners makes it even more difficult. There are many people who made this trip possible and helped along the way.

Above all I thank Fred Rohrbach, who traveled with me, for his time and efforts. Without him the idea for a book project on Vietnam would have been very difficult to bring to reality. Also thanks to John Rohrbach for his companionship on my second journey to Vietnam.

Then there are the many Vietnamese officials who helped us weave through the various layers of bureaucracy so we might accomplish what we had set out to do. Our first contact to Hanoi was Nguyen Van Quan, the Press Attache and Third Secretary at the Vietnamese Embassy in Bangkok, Thailand. His generous help was invaluable. Nguyen Quang Dy, Senior Press Officer at the Vietnam Foreign Press Center in Hanoi, is to be thanked for all of the time he spent helping us put the in-country logistics together. Duong Quang Thang, a press officer from the same office in Hanoi, was our constant Vietnamese companion, guide and interpreter. It was Thang who opened our eyes to the many wonders of Vietnam. His command of English made it possible for us to converse with the Vietnamese, get the right food, clean water and whatever else we needed. In Ho Chi Minh City, Nguyen Xuan Oanh, a former Harvard professor and now the nation's top economist and banker, spent hours explaining the current economic situation and future plans to us.

Several drivers worked with us during our stay in Vietnam but Nguyen Quang Hoa handled all the driving chores during our second stay, a trip covering about 2,800 miles. Hoa, a truck driver on the Ho Chi Minh Trail for nine years during the war, drove long hours without rest and sleep to meet our schedule.

We were warmly welcomed in all the provinces and cities of Vietnam and some of the names of our gracious hosts are: Nguyen Tai Cung, the Acting Director of Tourism for Vietnam; Van Nam, Director of Tourism at Haiphong; Nguyen Van Dieu, Chief of the Office of External Affairs for Binh Tri Thien Province, which includes Hue; Hoang Ngoc An, Vice-Director of Tourism in Da Nang; Pham Ngoc Hoa, Director of Tourism in Dak Lak Province and Buon Me Thuot; Nguyen Thang An, Director of Tourism for Phu Khanh Province and Nha Trang; Tran Trac, of the Department of Foreign Affairs in Dong Nai Province and Bien Hoa; Ngo The Dung, Director of Tourism at Vung Tau; and Duong Van Day, Director of Tourism in Ho Chi Minh City. These people treated us to dinners, saw to it that we had proper lodging and enthusiastically discussed their various regions with us.

There are many others whose names I cannot recall but whom I will always remember: the cyclo drivers in Hanoi and Ho Chi Minh City, those people who carefully did our laundry during our various stops and the people who made sure our meals were extra special.

Preceding Page: The Perfume River from the window of the Huong Giang Hotel on Tet morning. The mythology behind the naming of the Perfume River is that long ago a couple, very much in love and engaged to be married, were parted forever when the young man went off to war and was killed. His lover wept for a long time and eventually died. When she was buried a tree grew near her grave site that produced sweet smelling blossoms that fell into the river and floated south.

I would especially like to thank my young children, Todd and Kara Graetz, for their patience and understanding while dad was off traveling to a strange and distant foreign land. Not knowing anything about this mysterious Vietnam, but knowing I could not contact them, caused them constant worry until they finally heard from me at the end of each journey.

John Rohrbach, Nguen Quang Hoa, Duong Quang Thang, Fred Rohrbach, Rick Graetz

From a hilltop to the west of Pleiku looking northeast.

by Stanley Karnow

Vietnam.

The name alone evokes in Americans an assortment of feelings. It was to some a humiliating memory, the nation's first military defeat. To others it was a glorious crusade that failed for lack of determination. Still others, looking back in anger, denounce the involvement as a blunder. But a consensus nevertheless emerges from the spectrum of varied sentiments. Virtuous or shameful, commendable or misguided, sincere or contrived, the Vietnam war was a tragedy.

More than a decade since the dramatic end of the conflict, however, Americans are rediscovering Vietnam. Those who remember the ordeal are reexamining its causes, and many are revising their former opinions. Many, too young to recall it personally, are studying the experience as history. And out of the new perspectives, the United States has been learning, gradually and painfully, the limitations of its power.

Americans have not recoiled into isolationism. On the contrary, they are more aware of the world than ever before in their history. They realize, for example, that the U.S. economy depends on overseas trade. Surveys show that they would also support allies, such as Japan, Israel and the countries of Western Europe. But they are selective in their commitments. They are no longer comfortable in the role of global policeman. Nor do they still believe, as they once did, that America must spread its principles everywhere.

The roots of U.S. intervention in Vietnam reach back to what Professor Daniel Bell of Harvard has called America's concept of its own "exceptionalism." Early foreign visitors, like the French observer Alexis de Tocqueville, perceived in the United States an almost ideal society whose democratic institutions and individual opportunities ought to serve as model for decadent Europe, torn by poverty, frustration, class tensions and ideological turmoil. The idea of their own singularity inspired Americans themselves, and they began to believe that it was their duty to export their benefits to less-privileged civilizations abroad.

Thus, following the Spanish American war of 1898, President William McKinley decided to acquire the Philippines in order to "uplift" and "educate" the Filipinos…"and, by God's grace, do the best we could for them." Similarly, President Woodrow Wilson entered World War I "to make the world safe for democracy." The same theme resonated through President John F. Kennedy's inaugural address in 1961, when he pledged to "pay any price, bear any burden, meet any hardship, support any friend, oppose any foe, to assure the survival and the success of liberty."

America's intervention in Vietnam evolved from such vows. But the GIs who went there faced a formidable enemy. The North Vietnamese and

A private cafe in Ninh Binh south of Hanoi selling rice and pho, a white noodle soup that is essentially the Vietnamese national food. Com means rice.

Facing Page: *From the roof of the Palace Hotel looking southeast over Ho Chi Minh City.*

Vietcong were fanatically dedicated to the unification of Vietnam under their control, and they were prepared to suffer unlimited losses to attain that goal. So, while the United States won every battle, it was unable to achieve victory. Years later, former Secretary of State Dean Rusk admitted to an interviewer that he had "personally underestimated" the ability of the Communists to resist. "They've taken over seven hundred thousand killed, which in relation to population is almost the equivalent of—what? Ten million Americans?"

The nearly endless struggle in Vietnam gradually eroded the patience of Americans at home. They were accustomed to conventional conflicts, in which progress could be measured in terms of territory conquered. During World War II, for example, they could stick pins in maps and see victory ahead as the U.S. armed forces approached Germany or Japan.

The Vietnam war, however, was not a fight for territory. The United States pursued a strategy of attrition, hoping to break the morale of the Communists by killing their troops. But the enemy fought on and on despite horrendous casualties. And, after more than seven years, U.S. public opinion finally concluded that the conflict was not worth the investment. "Win or get out!" objected bumper stickers across America.

Probably no Americans are more sensitive to the dangers of a similar quagmire than U.S soldiers. They saw the armed forces of the United States demoralized and decimated by the Vietnam war. With their best battalions deployed in Southeast Asia, their responsibilities in Japan, Korea and Western Europe were weakened. At one point during the war in Vietnam, the only unit left to defend the continental United States was a brigade.

As a result, spokesmen for the American armed forces have made it clear that the U.S. military establishment does not want to became engaged again in a faraway place for an ambiguous objective.

Meanwhile, the Vietnamese are seeking a reconciliation with the United States. They came close to fulfilling that aim when they sought to cement diplomatic relations with the Carter administration. After months of talks, that effort failed, partly aborted by Vietnam's invasion of Cambodia.

Now the Vietnamese are trying again to bridge their differences with the United States, and their initiative is meeting a warm response from many Americans, among them veterans and even former prisoners of war. Several U.S. congressmen who have visited Vietnam feel that the time has come to heal the wounds of war.

Those wounds are dramatically visible in Vietnam itself, a lovely land whose people and landscape were devastated by a conflict from which they will take generations to recover. But, as they demonstrated during the war, the Vietnamese are indomitable and resilient—and they are bound to rebuild their country.

Increasing numbers of Americans will be traveling to Vietnam in the years ahead. Those returning will be able to to recognize its familiar sights and sounds and smells without the roar of cannon and the fear of death. For those going for the first time, it will be a voyage of discovery. For both groups, this book of extraordinary photographs is an introduction. And, as such, it dramatically illustrates a country that was—and remains—a symbol to Americans of an important chapter in their history.

Above: *A bomb crater used as a fish pond near the former DMZ.*
FRED ROHRBACH PHOTO
Facing Page: *Vietnamese cowboys in Da Lat.*

Saigon's last day…April 30, 1975…early in the morning a helicopter lands on the roof of the American Embassy. At 7:53 a.m. it is back in the air carrying the last of the embassy marines to the safety of the U.S. Seventh Fleet in the South China Sea. Twenty-one years of American presence in Indochina, which had at one time reached more than 500,000 military and civilian personnel, had just ended.

At 11:00 a.m. the same day Tank #844 flying the blue, red and gold colors of the National Liberation Front (Vietcong) broke through the gates of South Vietnam's presidential palace…the terminus of the Ho Chi Minh Trail had been reached. With the raising of the NLF flag, the Republic of Vietnam vanished into history. The war and almost 35 years of armed struggle and resistance, including combat with the Japanese and the French, came to a halt; Vietnam was soon to be unified as The Socialist Republic of Vietnam, and Saigon renamed Ho Chi Minh City.

Vietnam was quickly isolated from most of the Western Bloc nations. Although in-country strife had ended, troubles soon began with Khmer Rouge-led Kampuchea (Cambodia), and serious conflicts erupted with China, Vietnam's giant neighbor to the north. All three countries had aided one another in the wars against the French and Americans. The colonial era now ended, dormant and ingrained bad feelings resurfaced.

Clashes with Kampuchea over control of islands in the gulf of Thailand and their common border were fueled by new-found, assertive nationalism and age-old distrust between the Khmer people in Cambodia and the Vietnamese. The violent Khmer leader, Pol Pot, and his followers had been committing genocide in Kampuchea under a hideously misguided policy to create pure socialism instantly. Cambodia had fallen to the Khmer Rouge just 13 days before Saigon fell to the NLF and North Vietnamese. The Khmers' stated goal was to strengthen the country to face their enemy to the east; they considered it necessary for survival.

The Khmer Rouge attacked Vietnamese villages and massacred civilians. Both sides committed provocations and a war of propoganda ensued and intensified. On December 25, 1978 Vietnam launched a full-scale invasion of Kampuchea and by January 7, 1979 the Khmer communists were routed, and the capital, Phnom Penh, was occupied by the Vietnamese. A pro-Vietnam regime was installed, backed by a large military force to defend against the Khmer Rouge. This occupation has caused ill will toward Vietnam among some members of the international community, while others have supported its efforts to keep out the feared Khmer Rouge.

The Vietnamese difficulties with China were based on a similar deep-seated national mistrust, and each country looked at the other as a threat. Chinese army units conducted periodic raids on Vietnam's northern provinces. On February 17, 1979 the Chinese staged a massive and destructive invasion of these same areas and captured several provincial capitals before pulling back across the border. The purpose of the Chinese operation probably was symbolic, but both countries suffered heavy casualties in major battles with no clear victor. Domestic problems within China and Vietnam and internal ideological

From the top of the Palace Hotel looking at the pillbox-shaped former American Embassy building. It is from this rooftop that the last American Marines left early in the morning on April 30, 1975, Saigon's last day. The building now houses the National Oil and Gas Ministry.

Facing Page: *The One-Pillar Pagoda in Hanoi.*

15

A former Esso gas station in Da Nang, remnant of the American presence.

Facing Page, Top: The former Le Cercle Sportif, a French colonial sports club. It is now used for recreational pursuits of the workers. **Bottom:** In the Iron Triangle area.

strife within the Chinese Communist Party have probably prevented the conflict from escalating.

While these military encounters were taking place, Vietnam's leadership was struggling with the business of putting Vietnam back together and firing up its economy. The job of patching the war-torn nation was made almost impossible by an outdated ideology and the absence of competent people in key positions. Central planning and the end of the free-market economy in the south, combined with a lack of leadership, quickly put the already-dismal Vietnam economy on a rapid slide.

The Vietnamese politburo soon recognized that its success at fighting a war did not qualify it to run an economy. Its members listened to criticism of the banking system, and to those who advocated small-scale private enterprise and an open-door policy toward outside investment and tourism.

The December 1986 Sixth Party Congress generated a major shake-up brought on by severe criticism of the government. The hierarchy admitted its concept of socialism had been unrealistic and it allowed a more pragmatic leadership to be installed, headed by Nguyen Van Linh, the former party secretary in Ho Chi Minh City. The new Communist Party General Secretary and his supporters established a policy they call "doi moi," or renovation, which is along the Chinese model of reform. Mr. Linh began imposing on the north some of the more liberal political and economic reforms he had initated in the south while head of the party in Ho Chi Minh City. He bases much of what he is trying to do on his belief that it was wrong to dismantle private enterprise.

The December 1987 meeting of the national assembly took another major step forward when it ratified a new foreign investment code. This outward-looking policy allows overseas businesses to invest in Vietnam under favorable conditions, easy formalities and guarantees, including export of profits. The legislative body also realized that tourism is a quick way to bring more foreign exchange into the country. As a result Vietnam is beginning to make visas easier to obtain. Overseas Vietnamese are encouraged to return to visit, invest or even re-settle in their homeland. Almost overnight Vietnam has transformed itself from one of the most closed societies on earth to perhaps one of the more liberal of communist nations.

None of the above means Vietnam is now on a par with western nations nor do Vietnamese enjoy the freedoms of a democratic and capitalistic system. Hardly. Vietnam is a socialist country ruled by Marxist thought. Individual liberties are few and businesses must operate within the framework of a state-run economy. However, this Asian society is not a passive satellite of any communist power. Just as communism itself is changing in these days of *perestroika* in the Soviet Union and post-Mao reforms in China, so Vietnam is seeking its own way.

Vietnam has a long way to go before measurable improvements in its standard of living and overall economy are noticed. However, if its huge and entrenched bureaucracy does not hinder the new policies and attitudes, Vietnam's future could brighten. The jumble of government ministries and departments must be pared down and the reformers will have to remove road-blocks to progress. Many observers believe the programs now taking shape need to be even more cohesive and better coordinated. Time may prove that greater reforms will be needed for Vietnam to take part in the global economy.

First steps have been taken. What would help most would be normalization of relations with the west and, in particular, the United States. This Indochina

nation needs a massive infusion of hard currency, investment and western expertise that only good relations can bring.

While the Vietnamese heal themselves and search for economic vitality, people of the western world have the opportunity to see a most beautiful and intriguing land. Best of all, visitors will view a place that has yet to be spoiled by excessive tourism. Vietnam is very much Vietnam. Serious travelers can witness a culture and live with accommodations far different than they may find elsewhere. To be sure, improvements for the tourist are needed—there are no world-class hotels—and a lack of resources means upgrading will come slowly, but this is what makes Vietnam an adventure.

Vietnam: Opening Doors to the World will show off this country for what it is today. Fred and John Rohrbach and I were fortunate individuals. We spent a great deal of time in Vietnam during 1987 and again in early 1988. Our travels throughout the country totalled more than 2,800 miles. The visits covered areas not viewed by Americans before the war ended and, in some instances, places Americans may never have been, especially in the north. We wandered some of Vietnam's fabled highways, including National Route 1 from the north to the south. Along the way we took Route 9, which leads from the east coast of Vietnam inland to the border with Laos, as far as Khe Sanh. From near Qui Nhon on the South China Sea, well to the south of Da Nang, we climbed over An Khe and Mang Yang passes via Route 19 to the Central Highlands. The mysterious highlands were unveiled to us as we roamed down Route 14 from Pleiku to Buon Me Thout. When the roads ended we walked and took boats of one form or another, even floating a tributary of the Mekong River near Ben Tre to visit waterway settlements.

The war years gave the west a view of Vietnam as little but jungles and waterways. Our trip dispelled that myth. We discovered a splendid and incredibly diverse landscape and reached the conclusion that Vietnam is one of the most beautiful nations in all of southeast Asia: white, sandy beaches, serene seascapes, mountains, windswept plateaus, waterfalls, thousands of coastal islands, limestone islets with towering walls and caves and, of course, the jungles and rivers…they are all part of Vietnam.

Then there were the people. We were warmly welcomed to Vietnam by an extremely friendly, gracious and energetic population. In some of the places we visited, especially the highlands, we encountered folks, collectively called Montagnards, or mountain people, by the French, who seldom see foreigners. Vietnam has more than 60 ethnic minority groups, but Vietnamese constitute 90 percent of the country's population. Next most numerous are the Chinese followed by the Montagnards and the Khmer.

Very noticeable to us was the striking difference between the north and the south of Vietnam. It appears the country was unified in 1975 only politically and territorially. The lifestyles and dress of the people of the south, especially in Ho Chi Minh City, are a striking contrast to the north. Colorful clothing and far more economic activity and wealth are in evidence in the provinces around Ho Chi Minh City than throughout northern Vietnam. In essence two systems exist in one country. In the north, western domination disappeared when the French, whose influence had been felt since the 1850s, left in 1954. Rigid, hard-line communism filled the political void. The French as colonists, then Americans as allies to the Republic of South Vietnam, dominated the development of the south until 1975. The hard-line, puritanical, socialist mode of life became entrenched in the north, but the people in the south generally have

Above: *Market scene in Buon Me Thuot.*

Facing Page: *The mountain people, Montagnards to the French, a minority in Vietnam, near Khe Sanh along the Ho Chi Minh trail.*

tried to resist it. The way of life in the south, especially in Ho Chi Minh City, seems to be winning popularity elsewhere in the country. In addition, the weather in the north is harsher than in the south. South Vietnam experiences summer monsoons and has warm temperatures the year long; not only is Vietnam north of Hai Van Pass and Da Nang subject to a summer monsoon, but it also has several winter months of drizzly, damp, cold weather.

The distinctly Vietnamese way of life and the physical setting, together with the changing political situation, ensure a memorable and adventure-filled journey. Every encounter with places and people is fascinating. But it is the Vietnamese who make the place worthwhile to see. Their friendliness and helpfulness are genuine and their lives are easier to comprehend if you understand what they have endured. The cohesive family units and the way the children take care of each other could teach many other societies a lesson.

Memories and observations of our excursions to Vietnam will stay with me forever…visiting in Ben Tre with one of the leaders of the first armed rebellion against the government of South Vietnam in 1960…the hospitality of the local dignitaries at the seacoast town of Vung Tau…standing amidst the sandbagged bunkers and remnants of the war at the former outpost at Khe Sanh, where U.S. Marines were under seige for several months during the winter of 1968…crawling into the tunnels of Cu Chi and exploring the Iron Triangle area where some of the most fierce fighting of the war took place…walking along the now quiet Dong Khoi Street, which was once the wild Tu Do Street of Saigon and Vietnam war fame…running the route of the National Liberation Front and the North Vietnamese army tanks during the final moments of the war as they headed toward the presidential palace…photographing children and livestock along the banks of the placid Ben Hai River, once a no-man's-land known as the DMZ (Demilitarized Zone)…viewing the eerie prison on Hai Ba Trung Street in Hanoi that the American POWs dubbed the "Hanoi Hilton"…witnessing saddened emigrés prepare to leave Vietnam forever from Tan San Nhat Airport at Ho Chi Minh City…watching people perform incredibly difficult tasks in their everyday work…strolling beautiful, isolated tropical beaches on Vietnam's South China Sea coast…climbing Marble Mountain at Da Nang to survey a pastoral landscape that not too many years before had witnessed nightly mortar attacks…eating in small cafes while hordes of children and villagers stared as if we were on display…and most of all talking about peace and tranquility between nations with a people who want it…Vietnamese citizens.

Pictures and descriptions can only whet the appetite by serving as an introduction to a piece of geography. It is my hope that the magnificent scenery this book shows, mixed with the images of the people from all areas of Vietnam, and a brief interpretation of our own experiences, will entice you to visit Vietnam.

This book does not pretend to be a scholarly work or a complete dissertation on Vietnam. Its history is too long and complicated. With the exception of an occasional comment, I have stayed away from any major discussion of the country's politics, its socialist system and the war. Countless pages have been written about the Vietnam war and there are some outstanding historical accounts on the nation. My primary purpose is to show the beauty of Vietnam, describe a unique journey and give my impressions of the country. To understand Vietnam before the end of the war and for a glimpse into history, any book written by Bernard B. Fall is worth reading—and especially two of them: *Last*

Reflections on a War and *Street Without Joy. Brothers in Arms*, by Bill Broyles, Jr., provides excellent reading for those who served in the Vietnam conflict. And Nayan Chanda did an outstanding work titled *Brother Enemy: The War After the War*. His book tells what happened in the 10 years after the fall of Saigon including the intrigue among Laos, Kampuchea, Vietnam and China, and it covers in depth what I have briefly outlined in this introduction. It is an excellent work for understanding the current political situation in Indochina. Stanley Karnow, who spent many years in southeast Asia as a journalist, penned a masterful book called *Vietnam: A History*. If you can choose only one book to read on this nation, this should be it.

Other valuable reading on Vietnam includes *Decent Interval* by Frank Snepp, *The Tunnels of Cu-Chi* by Tom Mangold and John Penycate, *Vietnamese Tradition on Trial, 1920-1945* by David G. Marr, *The Ten Thousand Day War* by Michael McClear, *Dispatches* by Michael Herr, *Our Great Spring Victory* by General Van Tien Dung, *A Rumor of War* by Phillip Caputo, *55 Days, The Fall of South Vietnam* by Alan Dawson, *Giai Phong* by Tiziano Terzani, *The Lost Revolution* by Robert Shaplen, *Vietnam: Between Two Truces* by Jean Lacouture, and *Behind the Lines Hanoi* by Harrison E. Salisbury.

Rick Graetz
Helena, Montana
July 1988

The Vietnamese make use of practically everything. Here is the tail end of a rocket.

Facing Page: *Along the South China Sea looking toward islands off the coast of Nha Trang. Hon Tre is the largest island.*

Vietnam, occupying the eastern reaches of the Indochinese peninsula, is marked by an uninterrupted range of mountains and hills on the west and the South China Sea to the east. Its coastline is 3,000 kilometers (1,860 miles) long and its land border of 3,750 kilometers (2,325 miles) is shared with China, Laos and Kampuchea. From the country's northernmost point in Ha Tuyen Province on the Chinese border to the tip of Ca Mau in the south on the South China Sea, along an axis, is 1,650 kilometers (1,203 miles). By road on National Highway 1 from Hanoi to Ho Chi Minh City (formerly Saigon) is approximately 1,800 kilometers (1,116 miles). In some places Vietnam is only 50 kilometers (31 miles) across. The widest point, located in the north, is 600 kilometers (372 miles). The total land mass of the country is 329,600 square kilometers (204,352 square miles), three-quarters of which is made up of mountains and hills. The balance is coastal plain.

The country sits in the intratropical zone, between a latitude of 23 degrees, 22 minutes north latitude just below the Tropic of Cancer and stretches south to 8 degrees, 30 minutes north latitude, approximately the same latitude as southern Mexico and central Africa. Its longitude, not counting some of the outer islands, is 102 degrees, 10 minutes east to 109 degrees, 21 minutes east.

Above: *Fishermen in the South China Sea near Vung Tau.*

Facing Page: *Ninh Hoa, a small village north of Nha Trang.*

Vietnam's most prominent geographic feature is the Truong Son Mountain Range, the western backbone of the country. This system of alternate parallel mountain chains runs in a northwest-southeast direction, with an average altitude of 600 to 800 meters above sea level (almost 2,000' to 2,600' high). The slopes of the eastern Truong Son are steep while the western side has a more gentle grade that continues west into Kampuchea and the Mekong basin. The higher and steeper inclines of the eastern range constitute a climatic barrier. From July to January considerable rain falls here, but during the remainder of the year, the dry season, a foehn-type wind locally called the Lao wind, originating from the southwest, blows along these uplands causing extreme dryness and heat.

There are more than 200 rivers cutting through the mountains and many of them flow through deep ravines and narrow valleys leading to flooding during heavy rains.

Below an altitude of 800 meters (2,600'), the ground cover consists of a dense tropical rain forest, sometimes called a triple canopy jungle. Some of the trees grow to well over 120'. Evergreen forests begin to occupy lands above 800 meters. In these reaches some of the heaviest rains fall, amounting in some instances to more than 100 inches a year.

Vietnam's most diverse array of wildlife finds habitat in the Truong Son Range, including declining populations of elephants, tigers, panthers and deer. Scattered throughout the range in isolated

Above: *The parched, barren country northwest of Pleiku.*

Facing Page: *River scene near Cu Chi northwest of Ho Chi Minh City.*

small villages are minority ethnic groups—Montagnards (mountain people), as the French called them.

The highest peaks in Vietnam and in Indochina are in northern Vietnam in ranges separate of the Truong Son. Mountain masses such as the Hoang Lien Son chain consist of the loftiest peaks in the nation with many of them over 2,000 meters (6,500') high and some over 3,000 meters (9,800') high, including Fansipan, Vietnam's tallest peak, at 3,143 meters (10,312') high. The main segment of this range has inaccessible peaks with almost-vertical slopes and deep ravines.

The nation's most beautiful mountain passes are to be found in the coastal mountains. The most famous, Hai Van, crosses a range stretching toward the sea between between Hue and Da Nang. Ca Pass, just to the north of Nha Trang, and Cu Mong Pass, are also well known as is Phuong Hoang northwest of Nha Trang and Ngoan Muc, west of Phan Rang on the way to Da Lat.

The central highlands form another well defined physiographic area of Vietnam. In some respects the land looks much like the high plains meeting the Rocky Mountains in the United States. This high plateau can be best described as windswept, rolling and ringed by mountains. Its appearance is much different than any other part of the country. The earth consists of red basaltic material and although the region experiences a long dry season, it's still possible to grow tea, coffee and rubber. Pleiku and Buon Me Thuot are the two major towns in this sector. In Pleiku the plateau averages 700 to 800 meters of elevation (2,300'-2,600'); Buon Me Thuot sits at about 500 meters (1,600'). Although the entire highlands are relatively dry, the southern reaches experience less precipitation than farther north and vegetation, with the exception of a few pockets, is of the low-lying Savannah type. Mountains begin rising again in the southern end of the highlands and beyond. The resort city of Da Lat sits on another high plateau south of the highlands. At 1,500 meters elevation, (4,500'), Da Lat is in a region of pine forests and cooler summer temperatures than those found in the tropical Mekong and Saigon river deltas to the south. It was a vacation spot for the people of southern Vietnam seeking escape from the intense summer heat.

Coastal Vietnam may have one of the most varied and magnificent seascapes in the world. It consists of peaceful bays, beaches with surf varying from gentle to treacherous, limestone walls jutting out of the sea, sand dunes intruding on green rice paddies, and coconut palms and white sandy beaches. In some places mountain ranges end abruptly on the coast. In the Mekong and Saigon river deltas in the south and the Red River Delta in the north, the country is flat and used heavily for agriculture.

The coastal areas between 12 and 14 degrees north latitude, experience the driest climate in Vietnam, some places even have a desert-like terrain complete with cactus. Thuan Hai province to the south of Nha Trang is also a very dry area. The climate is classified as windy and semi-arrid; all that grows here is scrub.

Nha Trang and vicinity, located along the coast of Vietnam, is the gem of Vietnamese shoreline. The area is characterized by beautiful jungle-covered mountains, deep green rice paddies and aqua-colored bays. The climate is also among the best in the country. Nha Trang is a mecca for east bloc and in-country tourism.

The Mekong Delta, in the south, boasts the richest agricultural land in Vietnam as well as the hottest and most even climate. Temperatures in the sum-

In the rice paddies near Ha Long.

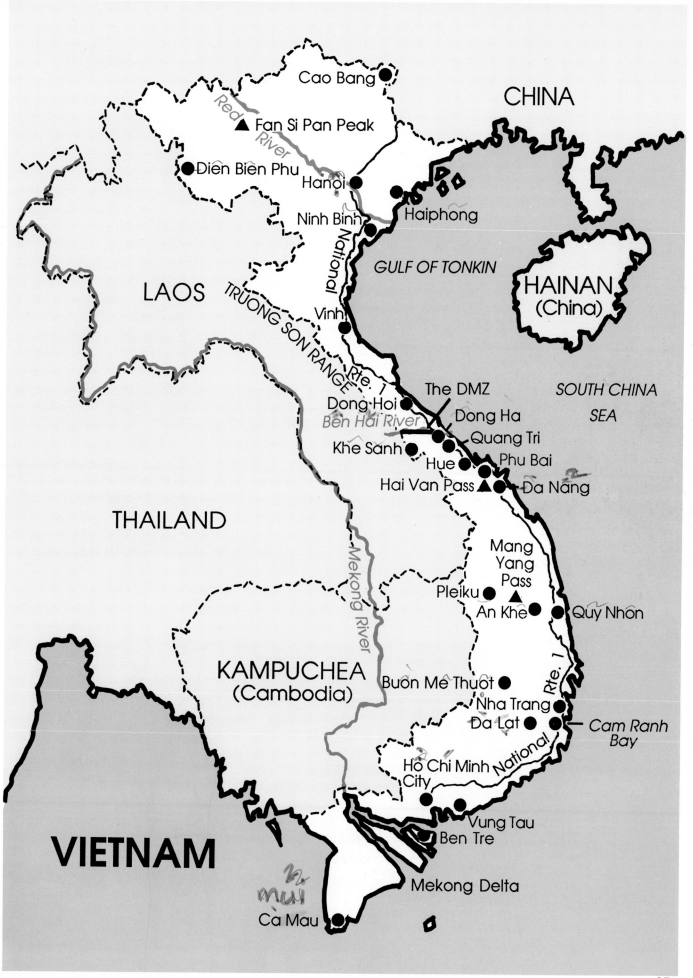

Cao Bang

CHINA

▲ Fan Si Pan Peak

Red River

Dien Bien Phu

Hanoi

Haiphong

Ninh Binh

GULF OF TONKIN

HAINAN
(China)

LAOS

TRUONG SON RANGE

National

Vinh

Rte. 1

The DMZ

*SOUTH CHINA
SEA*

Dong Hoi

Dong Ha

Ben Hai River

Quang Tri

Khe Sanh

Hue

Phu Bai

Hai Van Pass ▲

Da Nang

THAILAND

Mang
Yang
Pass

Mekong River

Pleiku

▲

An Khe

Quy Nhon

KAMPUCHEA
(Cambodia)

Rte. 1

Buon Me Thuot

Nha Trang

Da Lat

Cam Ranh
Bay

National

Ho Chi Minh
City

VIETNAM

Vung Tau

Ben Tre

Mekong Delta

mui

Cà Mau

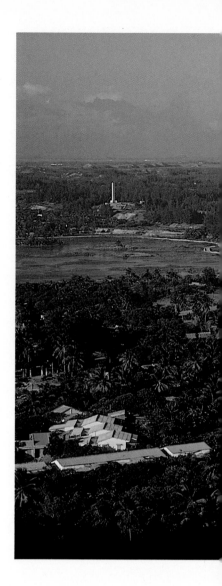

mer range to 100 degrees with very high humidity and in the winter season the lowest is in the high 70s. Much of the delta is covered with brilliant green rice paddies and orchards of coconuts, mangos, pineapples, bananas and oranges. The Mekong River is often referred to as the "artery of Asia." This river which is actually a braid of nine branches by the time it reaches the Mekong Delta of Vietnam, arises in the Himalayas of Tibet and drains parts of southern China, Laos, Thailand and Kampuchea. In Vietnam the Mekong River is also called the Cuu Long, which means "nine dragons."

Some of the areas of the delta not in agricultural production are marshes with mangrove growth. In the extreme southeast the U Minh Forest was well known during the resistance against the French and Americans. The Vietnamese call it "the sea of birds." This jungle marshland area is the second largest in the world after the equatorial mangroves in the estuary of the Amazon River. It produces very high quality wood.

Right: Looking over Vung Tau, a resort area used for in-country R & R by U.S. GIs. Approximately 72 miles southeast of Ho Chi Minh City, thousands of Vietnamese "boat people" fled from this coastal city during the last few days of the Vietnam conflict.

Below: Rice field workers at a cooperative between Long Thanh and Bien Hoa.

Ho Chi Minh City is located in the piedmont along the northern edge of the Mekong Delta and along the Saigon River.

In the north, the Red River Delta is also one of Vietnam's prime agricultural regions because of the rich silt soil the river brings down from China. It is also considered one of Vietnam's most important industrial areas. Hanoi, the country's capital and Haiphong, a very important harbor on the Gulf of Tonkin, are located in this geographic district.

Along the coast north from the Red River delta, limestone topography dominates. The far reaches of the northern coast are studded with thousands of islands and high mountains that rise from the shoreline. Most of the islands are 100 meters (330') high but exceed 400 meters (1300') high, presenting spectacular sights. Off of Haiphong Bay, a profusion of limestone mountains, many with cliffs, rise from the sea surface. The biggest of these mountain islands is Cat Ba, covered with dense vegetation, and with promise as a future resort area in the north.

Ha Long Bay, which means "landing dragon," just to the north of Haiphong, is a very special scenic area. The bay is dotted with hundreds of limestone islands of every size and shape imaginable. Some are sheer cliffs while

others are rounded vegetation-covered hills. Many of the islands feature caves and have great displays of stalactites and stalagmites.

Vietnam's population is estimated at about sixty million people with a high growth rate of about 2.61 people per thousand. Measures to control the birth rate have not been very successful as of yet, and a disturbing factor is that more than 50 percent of the population is under 21 years of age. Unless economic reforms bear fruit, this fact will present a huge problem in the not too distant future.

Above: *A sampan in Ha Long Bay.*

Facing Page: *The beach at Long Hai.*

From the moment we took off from Bangkok, Thailand on the Russian-built Hang Khong Vietnam (Air Vietnam) plane it was obvious we were heading toward a different world. The flight, lasting less than two hours, proceeds northeast from the Thai capital towards Udorn, Thailand, one of the bases during the Vietnam war from which U.S. planes staged their bombing runs over North Vietnam. Our flight path was much the same as theirs; the route crosses the Mekong River entering Laos, then up over the dense jungle mountains of Laos and into Vietnam airspace to the Red River Delta and Hanoi. A string of low mountains to the north of Hanoi become visible just before landing. This was the landmark for the fighter planes raiding the Hanoi area in the 1960s and early 1970s. American pilots referred to it as Thud Ridge, the nickname for the F-105 Thunderchief. Today, from the air, the only significant evidence of this devastating war in the delta region is the scattering of bomb craters now filled with water to serve as fish ponds.

In the midst of these ponds, surrounding rice paddies and small villages of the delta, sits Noi Bai Airport serving Hanoi. Its size and lack of significant activity suggest it is for a small city rather than an Asian capital. Bicycles move about freely on the tarmac almost without regard to landing planes, and here and there are stationed soldiers carrying AK-47 rifles. Off to one side revetments house Vietnam's MiG-21 warplanes. Inside the terminal, the air-conditioner and fans are turned on only when a plane arrives, which isn't often. The stern-faced immigration people, who look like army personnel rather than civilians, are efficient, and entrance into the country at the point of arrival is rather easy.

To drive the road into Hanoi, some 50 kilometers away, is a thrilling event the entire distance. Unlike western highways, the road is scattered with humanity rather than vehicles. The few in evidence are usually trucks and the narrow roadway necessitates some risky passing. As we had to share the limited space with walkers, people driving all sorts of livestock, children playing, bicycles carrying what would be a truckload of goods, and others engaged in various economic activities, the horn was constantly in use.

To see Hanoi is to go back to the 1940s; not much has changed except that its former beauty is now hidden. It has been described as having the elegance of a French provincial city in need of major repairs and a paint job. At night it takes on the appearance of a rural community. The few street lamps that work are dim, and the soft glow emanating from the sidewalks comes from kerosene lanterns and candles. On a clear evening the stars are brilliant; no pollution from bright lights or exhaust obscures them.

During the day, bicycles dominate and thousands of them hum on the pavement. Motor scooters dart in and out of the lines of cyclists and an occasional bus or truck spewing diesel smoke interrupts both with a loud horn. The taxis of modern cities are replaced by cyclo or pedicab drivers vying for space on the crowded streets.

Top: Road marker north of Hanoi installed by the French.
Bottom: The Red River Delta and rice paddies near the approach to Hanoi's Noi Boi Airport. The mountains in the distance were called "Thud Ridge" by U.S. pilots. They used them as a landmark for their bombing runs on the Hanoi area. Thud was the nickname for the F-105 Thunderchief.

Facing Page: Hanoi street scene.

Small coffee houses and private shops are sprouting throughout Hanoi. And although this is a socialist country, and the Russians have an enormous stake and influence in Vietnam, the popular music blaring from the cafes is western rock.

Most of the people seem to dress in the same drab clothing. The men wear green pith helmets and the women conicle hats called *non la's*. Lack of wealth appears to be evenly spread, although some individuals have more than others as evidenced by their newer bike or red Honda motorcycle and sometimes western dress. The few vehicles not owned by the government usually belong to foreign embassy personnel.

There are several places for foreigners to stay in Hanoi, but realistically only two are worth considering; one is the Thang Loi, better known as the Cuban hotel, positioned on the outskirts of the capital, or the Thong Nhat, the former Metropole Hotel located in the city center. Most tours groups are booked in the new hotel built by the Cubans, but the Thong Nhat is to be preferred. The old Metropole is steeped in history and located in the heart of Hanoi. This "inn" for foreigners leaves much to be desired from a standpoint of room quality, but the historical factors and location outweigh the concerns for western-style convenience. The Cuban hotel is an uninteresting structure with no access to cyclo drivers, thus limiting opportunities to move about and mix with the people.

The cost of eating in Hanoi is incredibly low, but, at this time dining opportunities are very limited. The hotel food is adequate but it is much better at the private establishments such as Cha Ca, the French restaurant, and 202. The restaurants are in the homes of the owners. With more free enterprise being encouraged, other places will no doubt open.

One of the most enjoyable activities while in Hanoi is to wander throughout the city on foot or by cyclo. An early morning visit to the food and flower markets for a breakfast of French bread and bananas is a special treat. After 6:00 p.m. in the old quarter of the city the many shops open and the crowds swell. Government workers earn after-hours income by selling almost everything imaginable, including black market goods. Wood and other carvings are good values.

Ba Dinh Square, the seat of the government of Vietnam, is the cleanest and best-kept part of the city. The Ho Chi Minh Mausoleum, Ho Chi Minh's house,

Below, Left: *Three cyclo drivers selling fruit on a Hanoi street.*

Right: *Hanoi cyclo driver.*

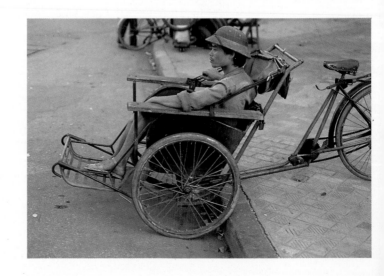

Left: *Selling fruit on a Hanoi street.*

Below: *Ho Chi Minh's house in Hanoi.*

the former French governor's mansion, the War Crimes Museum and the One Pillar Pagoda are all located here. The square is also the site for the occasional huge military parades communist nations are well known for.

For an overseas visitor nightlife in Hanoi is virtually nil. The one oasis is the Friday night gathering at the Australian Embassy's Billabong Club. English is the spoken language and the conversations become increasingly interesting as the evening wears on.

Jogging in Hanoi was easy. The Lake of the Returned Sword, just a couple of blocks from the Thong Nhat, provides an almost circular, one-mile track. Before 7:00 a.m., the lake shores buzz with activity. Vietnamese jog the course in everything but running shoes, men and women do Tai Chi and lively badminton games take place on the grass. It doesn't matter what the weather is, they are out every day. And the Hanoi weather is not the best. We were there in September and in February. September is the end of the monsoon season and the region can experience heavy downpours, hot temperatures and high humidity. In the winter months, especially January and February, more often than not the skies are gray and misty. And although the temperature is in the mid-50s, with the dampness it seems much colder. Other times of the year, especially in the spring months, this part of the north is intensely hot.

In Hanoi we first learned the value of British 555 cigarettes. For most Vietnamese it takes almost a month's wages to buy one pack. Although we aren't smokers, we purchased several cartons in Bangkok to use to open doors. Offering one cigarette often turns a difficult photographic situation into a simple one. And a full pack will do wonders. The Vietnamese are heavy smokers and the 555's are a status symbol.

Ho Chi Minh, or "Bac Ho" (Uncle Ho), is and was an intregral part of Vietnamese history, especially in northern Vietnam. To the Communists and those seeking unity for the country he was a revolutionary hero—the George Washington of Vietnam. Ho, an extraordinary man, dedicated his entire life to Vietnam and the unification of the nation. His picture and words are on enormous posters. The believers in the Communist cause carried his most famous saying with them in battle..." Nothing is more important than independence and freedom." He was basically a simple man who eschewed the trappings of power and refused to live in the former French governor's mansion. He felt it was too big for him, and besides he was fighting against what it stood for. It's doubtful non-Communists revere Ho Chi Minh; however, I've heard very few unkind remarks about the man. He was more a nationalist than a communist and no one has accused him of trying to export communism and revolution throughout the world. Americans with the Office of Strategic Services who knew him during World War II felt that if the U.S. government had worked with Ho Chi Minh as they recommended, the Vietnam situation would have never developed like it did.

From Hanoi we took a trip east to Haiphong and Ha Long Bay via Route 5. Hapihong, a port city, suffered through heavy war-time bombing. The most interesting sight is the harbor. Hundreds of small boats, some powered by paddles and poles, float alongside huge ocean-going cargo ships. We watched this activity from what the Vietnamese call a ferry. Vehicles, bicycles and people are jammed together on a flat barge pushed along by an aging tugboat that seems barely able to run. Every time we crossed a wide, fast-flowing river

Dong Xuan market in Hanoi.
FRED ROHRBACH PHOTO

on one of these, I wondered what would happen if the boat's engines quit running in mid-river.

Ha Long Bay, one of the north's major visitor attractions, features hundreds of dolomite formations rising out of the sea. Renting a boat to get a closer look is a necessity. Colorful sampans and various fishing craft ply these waters and add to the beauty of the setting. The city of Ha Long Bay has a decent hotel. We stayed in the more attractive older part, which looks like an old villa complete with verandas and a view of the bay. The newer structure appears more like a dormitory.

As one leaves Haiphong, the landscape changes from the flat river delta to mountainous terrain providing a contrasting backdrop to the vast farming collectives in the lower areas. Collectives have been a major cornerstone of the socialist system. Initially people worked the farms for the common good—that is, everything produced went to the state. Today, under the new policies, the farmers have to meet a government quota, the balance of what is produced may be traded on the free market or sold to the state, whichever will bring the highest price. Members of these collectives are given different-size plots depending on the size of their family. They tend to them after their work on the collective land is completed and they can grow anything they want for their own consumption, to sell on the free market, or to offer to the government.

Between Hanoi and Ha Long Bay there is very little evidence of war-time destruction. Some relics are visible here and there in the form of old French bunkers and bombed-out buildings. Even these are becoming fewer and farther between. Most buildings and bridges that were damaged have been rebuilt.

At Haiphong Harbor.

While driving between Hanoi and Haiphong a memorable sight is one of the trains pulled by a 1940s-era steam engine. Vietnam is one of the few places in the world where these classic workhorses are still in regular use. Smoke billowing out of the stacks gives warning of their approach; then the engine appears, usually decorated with people hanging on wherever they can find room and the engineers' bicycles tied to the front.

These steam locomotives illustrate just how the Vietnamese get every ounce of value from anything that can be driven, ridden, melted, bolted or patched. By some miracle or another they keep all their old cars, buses, trains and trucks operating and nothing goes to waste. Scrap piles last only as long as it takes to make use of each item in the heap. Their ingenuity and tenacity is incredible.

On our first trip to Vietnam we flew from Hanoi to Ho Chi Minh City. At flight time we were loaded on a small and ancient turboprop plane. With no FAA to make the rules, loading is a matter of cramming as many people and as much baggage and freight as possible into the plane. We were shuttled to a small rear cabin and the door was promptly closed. There are no smoking regulations, so the haze made it difficult to see the passengers across the aisle. And as it took some time to get the plane ready to go, it became suffocatingly hot and humid. Once in the air a cabin attendant came to the back and offered some weak tea and coffee. With people moving around and baggage teetering on the edge of

A steam locomotive north of Phu Ly.

Facing Page: *Ha Long Bay.*

Crossing the Dragon's Jaw Bridge, which spans the Ma River. In Vietnamese the bridge is called Ham Rong. Located some 160 kilometers south of Hanoi, it was a vital link for the North Vietnamese on National Route 1. The U.S. lost about 70 planes trying to take out the structure. Finally, in 1972, it fell to a laser-guided bomb.

the overhead bins, it was inevitable that she would bump someone or something so that this hot liquid would fall on somebody. As I was the largest person in that section, and offered the most body area, I was the target.

To begin our second journey to the south, we drove National Route 1. In the north, the road is in poor condition so it forced the driver to proceed slowly, thereby giving us a better look at the land and people en route. One of the more scenic spots was in the vicinity of Ninh Binh. The Vietnamese call this area "Ha Long Bay on the land." To the west of the city limestone towers rise in great profusion from the level plain.

Before and after Ninh Binh, we went through many small villages. In each, I was amazed to see the Vietnamese use of bicycles and buses. They place a huge load on the top and sides of the bike and stick a bamboo pole from the area of the handlebars and the seat so the rider who is now walking can stablize the bike. I witnessed what appeared to be pickup loads of goods on many of these cycles. Buses are the main mode of transportation for the Vietnamese. Almost every bus we encountered had people hanging on the front and back, sticking out the windows and sitting on the roof with assorted market goods and possessions, including chickens, ducks, bicycles and motor bikes. Sometimes the live ducks are tied by their feet and hung upside down on a rope that runs the length of the bus. Naturally they don't take to the procedure too well so the air is filled with quacking, screaming bus motors and the chattering passengers.

South of Ninh Binh, the road passes the city of Thanh Hoa and crosses the Ma River by way of the famous "Dragon's Jaw" or Ham Rong Bridge. This area was heavily fortified during the war and the U.S. lost about 70 planes before the vital bridge was finally knocked out in 1972 by a laser guided bomb. The defenders immediately built a pontoon bridge to take its place.

Vinh, the next largest city on the way, was largely destroyed during the war and since has been rebuilt with help from the East Germans. Driving through Vinh, I could not help but notice the plainness of the apartment buildings that look old before their time.

Just south of Vinh, a pontoon bridge crosses the Lam River. The former bridge was knocked out during the war and is being rebuilt. The crossing took us more than three hours. People from both sides in assorted vehicles, bikes, Hondas and on foot, were trying to get across this very narrow structure at the same time. In some places it became a stand-off and nothing moved until common sense prevailed and people began to inch across.

We reached the north-central coast of Vietnam above Dong Hoi. This is not ideal coastal real estate to the Vietnamese, but rather harsh windswept country. Sand dunes are encroaching upon the land, rendering agricultural activities almost impossible. If the Vietnamese can't grow something in an area they won't live there. This hard country has produced many of the country's revolutionary leaders.

Night was falling as we drove through this sparsely populated region towards Dong Hoi, our stop for the night. On the way we had to make a river crossing via ferry. It was pitch black and there were no fixed lights at the loading ramp to guide the boat. As I heard the ferry nearing the shore, a vehicle's lights were turned on so the captain could see where to land. The same operation was performed as we crossed to the other side.

Dong Hoi is just to the north of the former Demilitarized Zone (DMZ) at roughly the 17th parallel of latitude. This former boundary between North and South Vietnam generally follows the Ben Hai River. At one time it was mined

Apartments in Vinh built by East Germans.
FRED ROHRBACH PHOTO

and constantly bombed and shelled and anything that moved was fired upon. The area along the southern banks saw heavy mining, and although most explosives have been cleared, farmers occasionally become casualiies when their plows set off ordnance. The scene is now pastoral, with farming taking place on both sides of the river and children tending cows.

South of the Ben Hai River at Dong Ha, Route 9 branches off of National Route 1 heading west to Khe Sanh and beyond to the border with Laos. The mountains and valleys en route are beautiful, and Khe Sanh is a site of war-time significance. In early 1968, the U.S. Marines suffered through a brutal 77-day seige here. Remnants of the fighting, including a former outpost with its sand-bagged bunkers, rusting ammo boxes and artillery casings, are still very evident. What was once the major staging headquarters for the area is now a small town populated mainly by minority groups, and the former marine base is cultivated with coffee and pepper plants.

The Ho Chi Minh Trail was a myriad of pathways and roads leading from North Vietnam into Laos and then back to South Vietnam. It was used to bring supplies, weapons and troups to aid the communist movement in the south and much of the activity on the system was near Khe Sanh. Just east of the town a bridge crosses the Da Krong River leading to a branch of the trail that goes to the A Shau Valley. Some parts of the Ho Chi Minh Trail have been abandoned, but this section and others have been improved to create access to remote areas.

In the Khe Sanh area slash-and-burn agriculture is widespread. The government is attempting to discourage the practice and in many cases the people who farm in this manner are giving up their old ways and settling into the valley areas to grow cash crops.

Near the coast, Route 1 goes south to Hue, passing through the Quang Tri area where vicious fighting took place during the Vietnam conflict. A few tanks still sit alongside the highway. The next night's stop was Hue where we stayed at the Huong Giang Hotel on the banks of the Perfume River.

Hue is a good place to spend a few days as it is the former Imperial capital and the cultural center of Vietnam. The centerpiece of the city is the Citadel, a one-time enclave for emperors and mandarins, and home to Vietnam's last emperor, Bao Dai, who now lives in France. This structure, with 20- to 30-foot-thick inner and outer walls, is where the forces of the National Liberation Front and the North Vietnamese army were ensconced for more than 20 days during the 1968 Communist Tet offensive. Some of the fiercest fighting of these battles occurred in Hue.

We were in Hue as Tet began and the one-time commander of the National Liberation Front forces in the area of Hue to Phu Bai hosted a dinner for us. Tet is the Vietnamese Lunar New Year observed for at least three days beginning at the first new moon after January 20. It is the most celebrated holiday in the country.

Before leaving Hue we stopped to see the Khai Dinh Emporers Tomb and the Thien Mu Buddhist Pagoda.

From Hue, Highway 1 heads south to Da Nang. En route we viewed inviting isolated beaches, including Lang Co. Before reaching Da Nang, Hai Van, the most beautiful pass in Vietnam, must be negotiated. Old French bunkers remaining in the pass are silent tributes to a bygone era. Red Beach, just north of Da Nang and below Hai Van Pass, is where th U.S. Marines first came ashore in 1965 to begin an ever-building presence in the country.

Da Nang was a three-day stop and we opted for the Non Nuoc near Marble Mountain instead of a city hotel. It is in only fair condition but its location on "China Beach" makes it attractive. The beach was used for in-country R & R by the Americans.

Da Nang's waterfront and markets were interesting but what I enjoyed most was climbing Marble Mountain. The caves and the view from the top make the steep ascent worth it. It was a school holiday when we went up so the ever-present children tagged along in droves; a few even made it to the top with us.

During the war the enemy, hiding in the caves of Marble Mountain, mortared the U.S. Marble Mountain Airfield just to the north of the peak.

The market in Dong Hoi.

Facing Page: *Vehicles and people attempting to cross a bridge over the Lam River south of Vinh. The bridge had been destroyed during the war and its replacement is made of pontoons.*

In spite of the huge concentration of American troops in the Da Nang area, the National Liberation Front established a field hospital in the largest of Marble Mountain's caves. It was probably good strategy as no one expected it to be so close to the enemy. Today this cave serves as a Buddhist shrine and contains several large statues of Buddhas. A plaque denotes its former use.

Besides abandoned bases, some of the most visible signs of American involvement in Da Nang and other southern cities, are gas stations. Signs touting Shell, Esso or Caltex are still standing or hanging. A few stations are now used for government gasoline storage but others are deteriorating. There are no service stations in Vietnam as Americans know them. Instead, people buy precious black-market gasoline in recycled litre bottles from roadside vendors.

From Hanoi to this point, the scenery consisted of limestone formations, mountains, jungles and bamboo-type vegetation, interspersed with rice paddies. From Da Nang south, the tropical nature of the country begins to dominate and the scenery becomes more grand. South of Da Nang the Vietnamese call the landscape "the marriage of the mountains and the sea." Spurs of mountain ranges meet with the ocean surf. Coconut palms are everywhere and the beaches are inviting.

Beyond Da Nang, Route 1 passes through the town of Quang Ngai and the coconut palms of Tam Quan to the towns of Bong Son and Phu Cat. The Bong

Son Plains were significant during the war. Below Phu Cat and just before reaching the city of Quy Nhon, we turned west on Highway 19 and climbed to the Central Highlands, crossing An Khe and Mang Yang passes. The French suffered devastating military defeats in these areas. As the road gains elevation, the countryside makes a very abrupt change from lush, tropical lowlands with dense jungled mountains to a high, windswept plateau of red basaltic earth ringed by distant mountains. Population dwindles as agricultural production is limited. Pleiku is the stop for the night and, with no hotel in town, we stayed in a government guest house that at one time was a South Vietnamese general's villa. The place was in need of repairs but it was adequate for sleeping…that is until 4:30 a.m. when loud martial and exercise music, coming from the city square, woke us up.

The villa had been a sumptuous dwelling for these remote highlands. Probably U.S. and South Vietnamese military folks also used it at one time as there was a huge U.S. army map still on the wall.

Before leaving Pleiku we climbed the low hills to the west of town. They gave us good views into Kampuchea and pockets of light green rice paddies dotting the otherwise parched countryside.

From Pleiku it is 120 miles through the highlands south to Buon Me Thuot and en route the vistas are big and colorful. The central highlands are home to many of the minority ethnic groups. These minorities, or Montagnards as they're often called, speak their own dialects and often live separate of the Vietnamese with whom they have poor relations. Some of the tribes served as mercenaries for U.S. and South Vietnamese forces during the Vietnam war. They are now becoming a minority in their own areas as the central highlands are being resettled by Vietnamese who are enticed to come here from more heavily populated areas. This is done primarily to develop this area economically and lessen the influence of the independent-minded Montagnards. Recently-established rubber plantations on both sides of the road for many miles represent some of this activity in the "New Economic Zones."

The beach at Nha Trang. This area was a favorite in-country R & R site for U.S. military personnel, and the French also used it extensively.

Facing Page, Top: *The former commander of the National Liberation Front forces (Viet Cong) during the 1968 Tet Offensive in Hue.*
Bottom: *Along the outer walls of the Citadel at Hue. The walls are 20 to 30 feet thick.*

Early evening east of Pleiku.

We stopped at one of the villages to talk to the people but they were hesitant. They moved back to their houses and stared at us. Women smoked what appeared to be enormous cigars consisting of a tobacco leaf tightly rolled. They would help each other keep them lit by puffing while touching the lighted ends of each other's smoke. Many of the women had betel-juice-stained teeth, a sight I saw mostly in the older women throughout Vietnam. The betel nut, which they chew, supposedly gives a mild high.

Before reaching Buon Me Thuot the villages become farther and farther apart and the country appears almost desolate. The already-sparse appearances of vehicles fade to almost none. Valleys in the distance, such as Ia Drang, that once boiled over with war now are serene and sparsely populated.

We stayed in Buon Me Thuot for a couple of days. If it's not during Tet there is a chance to go to some of the smaller villages, such as Ban Don, and see

Market scene in Buon Me Thuot.

the elephants at work hauling logs. During the Tet period the animals are in the jungles resting.

Local officials led us on a trip to the Dray Sap, a series of beautiful waterfalls in the jungles just outside the city. The final eight miles to the area of the falls is a dirt road that has been established in the last seven years. It was a roadless region and a Communist forces encampment before April 1975.

Buon Me Thuot was the first major city to fall during the 1975 North Vietnam-National Liberation Front Offensive that led to the collapse of South Vietnam. The attack began at 5:00 a.m. on March 10, 1975, and within a few days the city was captured. A tank on display in a traffic circle in front of the Thang Loi Hotel, was used in that battle.

Off to the western horizon of Buon Me Thuot, the mountains along the border with Kampuchea look inviting but they are off-limits, probably for

Montagnard near Khe Sanh.

military reasons. Very few roads exist, so travel to this remote region where few people live is on foot or by elephant.

From Buon Me Thuot, Route 21 heads east toward the coast. As the elevation drops, the jungle coverage on the mountain slopes becomes dense. This is the true triple canopy: jungles with three layers of cover.

Before crossing Phuong Huoang Pass and near the town of M Drak, is a large concentration of Rhade minority people in small rural settlements of distinctive "long houses" built on poles. These people are part of a matriarchal society in which the older women rule the households. The younger women search for a husband and when they marry, the spouse and the daughter live in the mother's house. As the family grows, sections are added to each home, making them longer. The front and back of most houses have carved wooden steps. I was told the larger boards, or ladders, were for the matriarch and the smaller ones for the daughters. The stepladders in the back are used by the son-in-laws. The dwellings and the area around them appear to be quite neat. Pigs and other family animals stay underneath the house. Each individual family within the larger family group has its own living space and the dining and cooking areas are shared.

The road reaches the coast again to the north of Nha Trang at Ninh Hoa. Here mountains come almost to the seacoast and, with their lush green dark cover, blend in beautifully with the mint green or golden rice paddies and aqua ocean. Nha Trang deserves several days stay, not only to enjoy this, which many people consider the best area of Vietnam, but also for a chance to see the the Cham ruins and scramble around some of the countryside north to Ca Pass. Tre Nguyen Island off the coast of Nha Trang is also worth a trip and a boat rental can be arranged. One of the highlights of the island is the saltwater aquarium.

For body-surfing, Nha Trang, at times, provides some high and spectacular waves. Ocean enjoyment is enhanced here as this province offers some of the best weather in Vietnam. It has no long rainy seasons, and while the monsoons are drenching most of the country in the summer months, Nha Trang is usually sunny.

At Nha Trang the Thang Loi Hotel was our residence. If the names of the hotels sound familiar from city to city, it's not that they are like U.S chains. Rather the Vietnamese have renamed all their hotels either Thang Loi (meaning victory hotel), or Thong Nhat (which means reunification) or Hoa Binh (peace).

From Nha Trang and back on Route 1, the highway passes near Cam Ranh Bay. This was a huge U.S. Naval Base during the Vietnam War and now serves the same purpose for the Soviet Union.

Turning inland again south of Cam Ranh, Route 11 winds up and up to the spectacular Ngoan Muc Pass. The destination is Da Lat and enroute vegetation changes from tropical to pine forests. The town sits at approximately 4,500' and enjoys a much cooler climate than the hot, humid lowlands to the south and east. Many former French villas attest to the popularity of Da Lat as a summer retreat for the wealthy. Still, today, those who can afford it make a pilgrimage from the Ho Chi Minh City area and the Mekong Delta to Da Lat for vacations.

The old historic Palace Hotel still stands. And as at the Thang Nhat Hotel in Hanoi, I wondered what kind of stories the walls could tell. One of the waiters at the Palace had been there since the early 1940s and had seen some of history's better-known leaders such as Bao Dai, De Gaulle and Kennedy. His English was good and we learned much from him.

A long house of the Rhade people near M Drak.

The markets, lakes and villas in Da Lat are the most attractive sights.

South of Da Lat, the Bao Loc plateau drops off abruptly with the vegetation descending from conifer forests to dense jungles. After leaving the Bao Loc highlands the next objective in our odyssey was Ho Chi Minh City, formerly Saigon.

Saigon at one time was called "the Paris of Asia" and "the Pearl of the Orient." Vietnam war activities and a large foreign presence gradually eroded away that reputation. With the Communist takeover on April 30, 1975, Saigon became Ho Chi Minh City in honor of the deceased former president of North Vietnam. A large segment of the southern population still refers to it as Saigon. It was here that I often heard the phrase "after liberation," rather than after the war.

Although the political structure changed and some professions and activities were eliminated, the southerners didn't adopt the ways of the north. Dress is more fashionable and western mannerism is evident. Private economic activity, led by Chinese-Vietnamese, is commencing to thrive again.

On Friday and Saturday nights, much like their counterparts in America, Vietnamese teenagers "cruise the drag." Instead of driving cars they move in circles on Hondas and bikes. And although illegal, the prostitutes are returning and the black market trade is virtually in the open.

A young boy guarding his chicken along the south bank of the Ben Hai River, formerly the DMZ.

Facing Page, Top: Along Route 1 and the South China Sea south of Ca Ma Pass.
Bottom: Looking east in the southern part of the central highlands. Coffee plants are in the foreground.

Class differences are far more pronounced in the south. Expensive clothes, private vehicle ownership and the ability to dine at the good restaurants or attend the "Rex Nightclub" are the most telling signs. On the other end of the scale are the thousands of Amerasian children, sons and daughters fathered by long-gone U.S. servicemen, who are outcasts in their society. There is hope for them, though, as they are gradually leaving the country for the U.S.A. and elsewhere through the United States-sponsored Orderly Departure Program.

The better hotels in Vietnam are located in the former capital of South Vietnam. The Rex is perhaps the best, although the Palace, Majestic and Caravelle are also good choices. The Continental is being re-built. All of them now have Vietnamese names but the tourist officials and visitors still refer to them by their former titles. As in Da Lat, some of the waiters have been at the hotels since the 1940s and those who speak English have great stories to tell.

The food throughout the south, and especially in Ho Chi Minh City, is excellent, offering Vietnamese dishes and an abundance of seafood and tropical fruit in season. Even western food is available at the hotels and better restaurants. I recommend trying Maxim's on Dong Khoi Street, formerly Tu Do street, and Madam Dai's. Madam Dai's, a former law office, has only a few tables and dining takes place in the law library. The books are still on the shelves. Madam Dai, a lawyer with the opposition party under the former regime, and now a member of the National Assembly, sometimes abruptly appears to greet her customers. Maxim's is large and has a nightclub atmosphere complete with an orchestra. A private establishment prior to 1975, it is now state-owned.

One of the best occupations of time while in Ho Chi Minh City is to visit the countless shops and the Central Market. Handicrafts not found anywhere else are offered here. The most interesting are lacquerware and ceramics—and the lacqerware, considered the finest in the world, features inlays of mother of pearl and eggshell.

Cholon, the Chinatown of Ho Chi Minh City, and the former presidential palace, now called Reunification Hall, are fascinating places to visit. The government has preserved the palace as it was when South Vietnam fell on April 30, 1975. Other places to see include the former U.S. Embassy, now the headquarters for the national oil ministry; Le Cercle Sportif, a French colonial sports club still in use; the main Catholic church; Nha Rong Museum; and the Saigon River waterfront. Cyclo drivers are ever present, which makes it possible to avoid long walks between sights.

The tunnels of Cu Chi in the Iron Triangle is an interesting spot west of Ho Chi Minh City and will take about a day to visit. The Cu Chi Tunnels were part of what was estimated to be a 360-kilometer network of tunnels used during the war by the National Liberation Front. The Iron Triangle region saw constant fighting. At Cu Chi, the Vietnamese have set up a small museum with photographs, and a guide leads visitors to entrances to some of the tunnels for a chance to experience what life in the underground was like. Building this "underground city" was an incredible feat. Hospitals, school rooms, kitchens…they are all still intact. It was obvious to me, after trying to crawl in one, that they were built for much smaller people. The American "tunnel rats, who went into these subterranean passages to flush out the enemy had some terrifying moments.

We were able to spend a few days in the coastal city of Vung Tau, approximately 72 miles from Ho Chi Minh City. Many people consider this to be the

51

second-most beautiful-beach area in Vietnam. It was from these beaches that thousands of "boat people" fled South Vietnam as the Communists gained power.

The hospitality we received from the heads of the local government was outstanding. They housed us in a villa near "Pineapple Beach" that had belonged to a high official in the former South Vietnam government. From here we were able to explore the entire area, including the lighthouse hill above the city that commands a magnificent view of Vung Tau and seemingly endless miles of coastline along the South China Sea.

Another day trip, or an over-nighter for a small group (accommmmodations are limited), is to Long Hai, a beautiful undeveloped beach region north of Vung Tau. The province officials here have high hopes for their area in the future but, right now, most of the beaches are occupied only by a few fishermen.

As is the case throughout Vietnam, the major activity in the fields or paddies between towns such as Vung Tau, Ho Chi Minh City and Long Hai is rice growing and harvesting. The lack of modern machinery brings the threshing operation to the roadway. The workers spread the straw on the road and the rice is threshed by cars and trucks driving over it. The highways are also used for drying the rice once it is threshed.

Returning from Long Hai to Ho Chi Minh City we drove past the former Long Binh Army Base, one of the United States' largest in Vietnam, and through the city of Bien Hoa. Today the old Army base is a ghost of its former self. All that remains are acres of concrete slabs and roads interspersed with eucalyptus trees planted in recent years.

Ben Tre, several hours out of Ho Chi Minh City, was the last side trip of our journey. The province and city are significant to some Vietnamese as the site, in early 1960, of the first armed resistance against the Diem regime that controlled South Vietnam, and the National Liberation Front was organized here.

To reach Ben Tre, a long ferry crossing of the Mekong River is required. The ferry leaves My Tho and proceeds downriver before reaching the other side. En route, the boat goes partially around Phoung Island. This was home for 10 years, beginning in the mid-1960s, to the Daoist coconut peace sect. The guru, Dao Dua, was better known as the coconut monk. He mysteriously disappeared in 1974. Members of the sect lived on coconuts and fruit and built many strange sculptures, including metal towers. The area now appears as an abandoned rusty amusement park.

It was about Ben Tre, which was totally destroyed, that an American officer made the comment, "It became necessary to destroy the town in order to save it." Ben Tre requires an overnight stop. The local People's Committee

Ho Chi Minh City street scene.

Facing Page: *From the roof of the Rex Hotel looking toward the Plaza Hotel. This street leads to the Saigon River.*

SƠ ĐỒ HỆ THỐNG ĐỊA ĐẠC CỦ CHI

ĐỊA ĐẠO CỦ CHI
TRONG BÁO CÁO CỦA ĐẠT-MO-LEN
GỬI TỔNG THỐNG MỸ

Above: A painting depicting the famous tunnels of Cu Chi. This elaborate system of tunnels led to underground hospitals, schools, eating areas, meeting rooms and sleeping quarters and is said to have extended 360 kilometers (216 miles).

Bottom Drying rice on the road near Hoc Mon. Farmers spread the rice husks to be broken by passing vehicles.

arranged for a half-day trip on one of the branches of the Mekong River. Traveling on the river opens up areas not accessible by road. The small waterway settlements and locals moving about provide excellent photographic opportunities. And the hot steamy swamps made me appreciate the hardships men and women who fought here experienced.

We were in the south in September and again in February and noticed a marked difference in weather from the north. The northern part of the nation is subject to prolonged cloudy periods during the summer monsoon and in winter. The south experiences much more sun and can be brutally hot. The only daytime respite comes from the build-up of monsoon clouds. In winter the sun holds sway most of the time. Even during the monsoon season it doesn't rain every day. The more likely pattern is an afternoon build-up of towering clouds, a downpour and a clear humid evening. True tropical weather.

Tan San Nhat Airport, outside of Ho Chi Minh City, was one of the busiest airports in the world during the war. Today it is quiet only by comparison. My two Air France trips out of Vietnam left from here. Each time the place was bustling with activity. What caused much of the commotion was a sight of sadness and happiness. Hundreds of Vietnamese who had been granted exit visas through the Orderly Departure Program were preparing to leave their homeland.

Many were Amerasia children going on to a better life in the free world. Others were leaving to join relatives and family members who may have been amongst the boat people and other refugees who fled the 1975 Communist takeover. Emotions ran high… crying, sad looks, empty stares and fear…both from the people leaving and from those who had come to see them off. Vietnam, as delightful as it is to visit, isn't a place where everyone can comfortably stay.

I've left one of the most interesting phenomena about our visit to Vietnam to the last. If you've ever wondered what it is like to be watched like an animal in a zoo, Vietnam is a good place to experience it firsthand. It has one of the highest birthrates in the world, so children are everywhere. The few foreigners they have seen mostly

Late afternoon from the Majestic Hotel looking east to the Saigon River.

are Russians, whom they taunt by shouting Lien Xo (pronounced *lin so*). They like to tease the Russians by referring to them as Americans without dollars. I quickly learned to say *khong phai lien xo…toi nguoi my* (I am not a Russian…I am an American.) Occasionally that would garner an amazed look and then the response "U.S.A. number one." More often than not they laugh or stare at this creature from outer space.

The most memorable incidents for me were when photographing or walking down the road. The longer I stayed in one place, the more children gathered. Many times when I walked through small villages taking pictures, before I knew it several hundred children were following me. What was most unnerving though was standing on narrow bridges with children crowding around, reaching up to block my view of pictures. To them it was funny and to the adults watching it, amusing.

In the smaller communities, we ate in little cafes that had only two or three tables. By the time we were ready to eat our food it seemed the entire village was gathered around the place watching us eat.

A word of caution. Don't attempt to give out candy or any other item to the children. You'll never have enough and you'll be hounded until you leave.

Two other things about Vietnam are worth mentioning.

In Vietnam the national dish is pho (pronounced *fuhh* drawn out). Pho is a white noodle soup, and chicken (Pho Ga) or beef (Pho Bo) can be added to it. It is commonly eaten for breakfast but is available for any meal. I enjoyed it at lunch almost every day.

Vietnamese men have an old and venerated custom of holding hands. During the war, Americans not understanding this, misinterpreted it as gay behavior. It is all part of the closeness these people have for families and friends.

If extra time is available, I recommend some other areas to add to an overall trip. From Hanoi, go north to Cao Bang and the Vietnamese-Chinese border, an area of many limestone formations and mountains. If transportation can be arranged, Tan Trao, also north of Hanoi, is another historical sight. This is where Ho Chi Minh returned to Vietnam after 30 years absence and began his struggle against French colonialism. To the west of Hanoi and along the Laos border, an even more difficult place to reach is Dien Bien Phu. This is the mountainous region where the Viet-Minh forces overwhelmed the French in the spring of 1954 to bring a close to the French-Indochina war. It was shortly thereafter that the Geneva Accords were signed and northern Vietnam gained independence from France.

The itinerary I've listed above, without the extras, might take more than a month, perhaps five weeks is better. I saw most of Vietnam over the period of two trips and had plenty of time. If you do not have four or five weeks then it is possible to fly to a few key areas such as Da Nang from Hanoi and then take a side trip to Hue. By flying to Ho Chi Minh City from Da Nang, you can visit the south including the beaches of Vung Tau and possibly Nha Trang.

This description of our journey and suggestions for others, is based on the experiences of three of us traveling Vietnam on a government-approved project; we went as journalists to complete a book on the country. At this time individual tourists cannot travel the way we did. Use this information to work with a tour operator who can arrange a trip, or keep it for a time, which may not be in the too distant future, when individuals can visit Vietnam as independent travelers.

Above: *Water for an old car.*

Facing Page: *The "Front Beach" at Vung Tau.*

Following Page: *Boats under construction at Long Hai.*

Above: Hanoi Street Scene.

Right: The tail section of an American B-52 plane shot down during the Vietnam conflict in a fish pond near a school in Ngoc Ha, a suburb of Hanoi. This plane was downed on December 27, 1972, and was one of 23 B-52's the Vietnamese claim they knocked out of the air.

Facing Page, Top: Hanoi during Tet. The trees and orange bushes are to Vietnamese as Christmas trees are to Westerners.

Facing Page, Bottom: A barber on Hanoi street.

NORTH

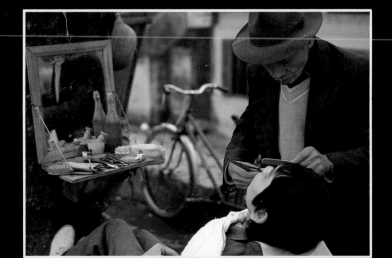

Left: *Along the banks of the Red River.*

Above: *The banks of the Red River in Hanoi. The Paul Doumer Bridge is in the background. This bridge was knocked out or cut in half by bombing but was quickly rebuilt.*

Facing Page, Top: *Ho Hoan Kiem (Lake of the Returned Sword).*

Facing Page, Bottom: *The government bank in Hanoi and a portrait of Ho Chi Minh.*

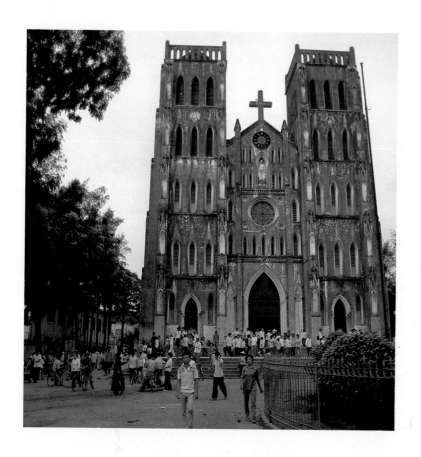

Left: *The Catholic Church in Hanoi built by the French. Mass is still celebrated here.*
Below: *Hanoi street scene and Ho Hoan Kiem (Lake of the Returned Sword).*

Facing Page, Top: *The former French Governor's palace at Ba Dinh Square in Hanoi. Ho Chi Minh refused to live in this and instead a simple dwelling in the back of the palace was built for his residence. He believed that he should not live in such elaborate comfort when he was fighting against the French and their colonial excesses. He also believed the mansion was too big for him.*
Facing Page, Bottom: *The former French opera house in Hanoi.*

Above: *Selling shoes on a Hanoi street.*
Above, Right: *Hanoi children.*
Right: *Changing of the Guard at the Ho Chi Minh Mausoleum in Ba Dinh Square, Hanoi.*

Facing Page: *A sampan in Ha Long Bay.*

Above: *A woman harvesting food for pigs.*
Right: *Carrying vegetables to market along the route between Hanoi and Haiphong.*

Facing Page, Top: *Water buffalo boys in the rice paddies.*
Facing Page, Bottom: *Irrigating the rice paddies.*

Above: *A small village in the Hon Gai coal mining area north of Ha Long.*

Facing Page: *Carrying wet sand for a brick making-project east of Hanoi.*

Right: *A 1940's vintage steam engine approaches the Dragon's Jaw Bridge coming through the town of Thanh Hoa. This area was evacuated during the bombing raids and much of the town was destroyed.*

Below: *Women carry chunks of coal for home use from the coal yards near Ha Long Bay.*

Facing Page, Bottom: *Making bricks north of Hanoi.*

Left: *A family on the road south of Vinh.*
Below: *A people-and-vehicle jam approaching a pontoon bridge crossing the Lam River south of Vinh.*

Facing Page, Top: *Paper flowers.*
Bottom: *Crossing the Lam River south of Vinh.*

Above: *Re-education camp guards at the Nam Ha camp in Ha Nam Ninh province south of Hanoi.*
Left: *Carrying wood in the mountainous area south of Hanoi and near Phy Ly.*

Facing Page: *Along the banks of the Red River, a child eats her lunch.*

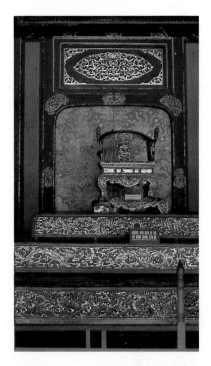

Left: *Outer walls of The Citadel and Hue. The Citadel was home to Vietnamese emperors. The Mandarins and educated people lived between the outer and inner walls; the Emperor lived inside the inner walls. Today people live within the walls and it has become a small village with much gardening taking place.*
Above: *The Emperor's throne in the Citadel in Hue.*

Right: *The Vietnamese flag flys over The Citadel at Hue.*
Below: *The Emperor's tomb southwest of Hue.*

Facing Page, Top: *The Perfume River at Hue.*
Facing Page, Bottom: *A scene along Le Loi street in Hue, the site of some of the fiercest fighting of the Tet Offensive in 1968. U.S. Marines literally fought house-to-house in this sector of the city.*

Above: *The Thiên Mụ Buddhist Pagoda in Hue built in 1619. This is the center for Buddhism in central Vietnam.*
Facing Page: *The Perfume River at Hue.*

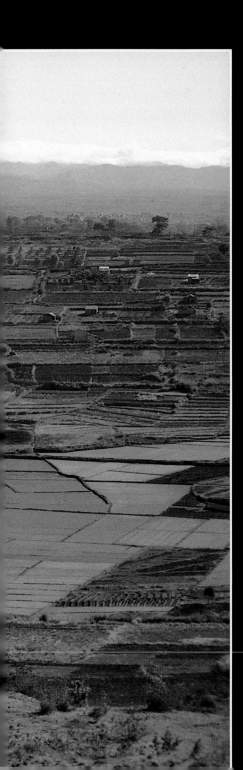

MANG YANG PASS

PLEIKU

AN KHE

BUON ME THOUT

CENTRAL HIGHLANDS

Below: *The "Rock Pile" at Khe Sanh.* KEN WOLFF PHOTO

Facing Page: *From a hilltop west of Pleiku looking east.*

Left: *Rice paddies in the highlands beyond Mang Yang Pass.*
Below: *Looking southeast from Mang Yang Pass.*

Facing Page, Left: *A Catholic Church at An Khe.*
Facing Page, Right: *Coming into the town of An Khe. Toward the hilltop in the distance was the site of a helicopter base for the First Air Cavalry Division in this area.*
Facing Page, Bottom: *Looking into the highlands from approximately 30 miles north of Quy Nhon.*

Top, Left: *A loaded bus on Route 14 to Buon Me Thuot.*

Top, Right: *A remnant of a former time along Route 14. Saigon has since been renamed Ho Chi Minh City. The distances are in kilometers.*

Below: *The central circle in Buon Me Thuot. Buon Me Thuot is a strategic town located in the central highlands and it was the first major city to fall in March 1975 as the North Vietnamese and National Liberation Front forces began their final offensive.*

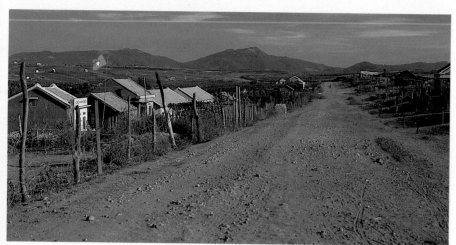

Above: *Young rubber trees in the highlands off of Route 14 to the south of Pleiku.*
Left: *A windswept scene on the outskirts of Pleiku.*

Left: *Montagnard women smoking.*
Below: *Jungle vegetation on the road between Buon Me Thuot and the coast and just below Phuong Hoang Pass.*

Facing Page, Top: *The Dray Sap waterfalls to the southwest of Buon Me Thuot in the jungles.*
Bottom: *Examples of slash and burn agriculture practiced by the hill tribes.*

Right: *Making sugar cane drink in Buon Me Thuot.*

Below: *A street vendor in Buon Me Thuot.*

Facing Page: *A python along Route 21 in the Central Highlands.*

Right: Minority people to the east of Buon Me Thuot.
Below: A Rhade village and its distinctive long houses in the central highlands near M Drak.

Facing Page: An Rhade family.

CAM LO
THE DMZ
DONG HA
QUANG TRI
HUE
PHU BAI
DA NANG
KHE SANH
CHU LAI
HAI VAN PASS
MY LAI
QUANG NGAI
QUI NHON
NHA TRANG

CENTRAL

Above, Right: *A woman with her ducks in Dong Ha.*
Below: *The Gio Linh Bridge over the Ben Hai River, which formed the demilitarized zone, DMZ, the dividing line between North and South Vietnam.*
Facing Page, Top: *The village of Khe Sanh from the outpost.*
Facing Page, Bottom: *Ben Hai River.*

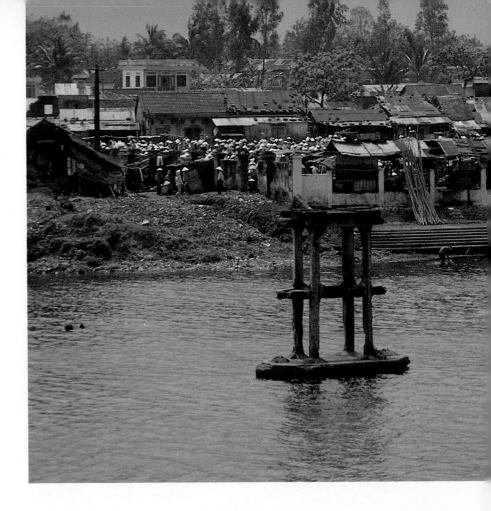

Right: *A market scene at Dong Ha on the banks of the Dong Ha River.*
Below: *From an outpost looking northeast at the area around Khe Sanh.*
Facing Page, Bottom: *The mountains below Khe Sanh.*

Right: *Along Route 9 to Khe Sanh.*
Below: *From an outpost looking toward Laos. This was one of the outposts for the U.S. Marines at the time they suffered through a long seige during February of 1968. The South Vietnamese Army may have also used this hill. The many bunkers with sandbags are still in place. The structures in the middle of the photograph are the start of a memorial to North Vietnamese soldiers who were killed in the war.*
Facing Page, Top: *Mountain people along the former Ho Chi Minh trail near Khe Sanh.*

Facing Page, Bottom Left: *From the outpost looking south to the jungled mountains from which much of the artillary fire and attacks were coming during the seige of Khe Sanh.*
Facing Page, Bottom Right: *Slash and burn agricultural practices in the jungled mountains near Khe Sanh.*

Right: *Resident of Dong Hoi.*
Below: *Part of the Ho Chi Minh trail, which was actually a series of trails leading from the north through Laos, bringing supplies and troops into South Vietnam. This segment of the trail is near Khe Sanh and has been paved. We crossed the Da Krong River to reach it.*

Facing Page: *Vegetation on the south slopes of Hai Van Pass.*

Left: Former French bunkers in Hai Van Pass north of Da Nang.
Below: Rice paddies and mountains to the north of Da Nang.

Facing Page, Top: A woman walking along "China Beach" at Da Nang. This was a site of in-country R & R for American military personnel.
Facing Page, Bottom: Descending Hai Van Pass looking north along the sea coast at the cloud covered mountains.

Left: *From the top of Marble Mountain looking north at the site of the former Marble Mountain airbase. The potholes in the background are a result of shelling.*
Below: *An early evening scene east of Pleiku.*

Facing Page, Top: *From the top of Marble Mountain looking north.*
Facing Page, Bottom: *Marble Mountain to the south of Da Nang. Marble Mountain consists of many caves in which the National Liberation Front forces hid and shelled U.S. military.*

Right: *A street market scene in Da Nang*
Below: *The harbor in Da Nang. The water tower in the distance on the left of the photograph is the former site of the American naval base.*

Facing Page, Top: *A beach scene along the China Sea near Sa Huynh.*
Facing Page, Bottom: *In the Bong Son Valley.*

Right: *Near Nha Trang, a farmer herds his ducks.*
Below Left: *Rice paddies and mountain ranges in the mist of Nha Trang.*
Below Right: *Sand dunes from the ocean meet rice paddies south of Ca Ma Pass.*
Bottom: *A bay to the north of Nha Trang.*

Above: *A beach scene north of Nha Trang.*
Left: *A fishing village north of Nha Trang.*

Left: *A Vietnamese "car wash" just to the east of the highlands near Ninh Hoa.*
Below: *A flower garden along the coast north of Nha Trang.*

Above: Nha Trang.
Right: Da Lat townsquare. Da Lat was and still is a favorite resort for the people living in the hot, humid lowlands to the south. At approximately 4,500 feet of altitude, it is relatively cool, even summer.

Left: *The town square in Da Lat.*
Below: *Da Lat.*

Top: *The Da Lat Palace Hotel.*
Above Left and Right: *Former French villas in Da Lat.*

Facing Page, Top: *Bananas having arrived via bicycle.*
Bottom: *A water wheel at work in the mountains of the southern highlands.*

Above: *A small village at the foot of Bao Loc Pass on Route 20 heading south.*
Facing Page, Top: *Tea growing toward the horizons in the highlands of the Bao Loc Plateau. The scene is from Route 20.*
Facing Page, Bottom: *Looking west on the southern edge of the Bao Loc Plateau.*

Above: *Street scene in Nha Trang,*
"Cho-Tet, 1988."

Facing Page, Top: *A small village*
at the foot of Bao Loc Pass on Route
20 heading south.
Facing Page, Bottom: *A Citroen*
taxi loaded with people and bicycles on
its way from Bien Hoa to Ho Chi
Minh City.

Right: *From the highest point above Vung Tau looking to the South China Sea. This photograph was taken from a French lighthouse built in 1908. It is falling into decay, but still in working order.*

Below: *On a tidal river flowing toward Vung Tau and the South China Sea.*

Facing Page, Top: *Cattle being driven along a road near Vung Tau.*

Facing Page, Bottom: *Farmers working the rice paddies along the road to Vung Tau, near the village of Long Thanh.*

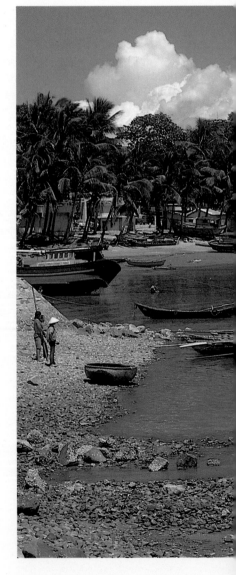

Above: *Coastline at Vung Tau.*

Facing Page, Top Left: *"The Back Beach" at Vung Tau.*
Facing Page, Top Right: *On "The Front Beach" at Vung Tau.*
Right: *Boats in one of the bays at Vung Tau.*

Left: *A statue at the Buddhist Taigung Lam Pagoda. This pagoda is in Dong Nai Province east of Ho Chi Minh City.*
Below: *An "elder statesman" at the Dai Lam Pagoda, erected in 1969 in Vung Tau.*
Bottom Left: *Buddhist monks at the Dai Lam Pagoda.*
Bottom Right: *Inside the Dai Lam Pagoda.*

Facing Page: *In the Taigung Lam Pagoda.*

SOUTH

Left: *Rice paddies west of Nha Trang.*
Below: *A woman untying her ducks.*

Right: *Nha Trang.*
Below: *Nha Trang.*

Facing Page, Top: *The Buddha in Nha Trang.*
Facing Page, Bottom: *Cham ruins in the Ba Thap region just south of Cam Ranh Bay. These ruins are relatively well preserved since they are inland and not affected by the ocean salt.*

Above: *Flower market in Nha Trang.*
Facing Page: *Cham ruins, which date from the 8th or 9th century, in Nha Trang.*

Right: Cham people.
Below: Cham people.

Facing Page, Top: Heading up
Ngoan Muc Pass on Route 11 on the
way to Da Lat.
Facing Page, Bottom: This area
near Phan Rang is considered to be
one of the dryest regions of Vietnam,
as evidenced by the cactus.

Facing Page, Top Left: *From the roof of the Rex Hotel looking toward the Caravelle Hotel.*
Facing Page, Top Right: *From the roof of the Rex Hotel looking at one of the main streets of Ho Chi Minh City.*
Facing Page, Bottom: *From the roof of the Palace Hotel looking to the southeast over Ho Chi Minh City.*

Below: *The City Administration Building, Ho Chi Minh City.*

Below: *Van Lang Catholic Church on the outskirts of Ho Chi Minh City. The former president, Ngo Dinh Diem, and his brother hid in this church while negotiating their surrender during the military coup that ended their regime in November 1963. They were picked up from the church by a junior officer, placed in an armored personnel carrier and shot outside of the city.*

Below Right: *The central market in Ho Chi Minh City.*

Facing Page Top: *This building housed the congress of the government of South Vietnam before. It is now used for a theater. The cement statue base was a monument to South Vietnamese Marines and was torn down when the National Liberation Front and the North Vietnamese Army came into Saigon.*

Above: *A street scene in Cholon district of Ho Chi Minh City. This area is also called Chinatown.*

Facing Page, Top Left: *Inside the presidential palace. The government of Vietnam has preserved the furnishings. This is said to be the room in which General Duong Van Minh waited to surrender South Vietnam to the commanding general of the North Vietnamese forces in the area. Minh had taken over as president during South Vietnam's last days after President Thieu fled the country.*
Top Right: *Inside the presidential palace where President Thieu met with foreign dignitaries. For the most part this was his office.*
Botom: *Local militia marching in front of the former presidential palace. On the morning of April 30, 1975, a North Vietnamese tank manned by the National Liberation Front (Viet Cong) broke through the gates in front of the palace bringing an end to the Vietnam War. Within moments, they had raised the National Liberation Front flag.*

Above: *Early in the morning looking toward the southeast from the Majestic Hotel at the Saigon River and port.*

Top: *Looking northeast from the Majestic Hotel on the Saigon River.*
Above: *The Mekong River at Ben Tre.*

Right: To the north of Cu Chi along the Saigon River. This is one of the points where the tunnel users submerged to enter the tunnels.
Below: A river scene near Cu Chi northwest of Ho Chi Minh City.

Left: *Washing clothes near Hoc Mon.*
Below: *A river scene near Cu Chi northwest of Ho Chi Minh City.*

Left: *Rice workers in the Cay Lay district of Tien Giang province.*
Bottom Left: *Road work near My Tho Tien Giang province.*
Bottom Right: *A waterway near Ap Bac village. In 1963, a major battle raged here between the South Vietnamese Army and the National Liberation Front.*

Facing Page, Top: *On the Mekong River at Ben Tre. The Ben Tre area witnessed the first armed uprising against the Diem regime in January of 1960, thus starting the American era of the Vietnam conflict. The National Liberation Front was founded here in 1960.*
Facing Page, Bottom: *Road work near My Tho, Tien Giang province.*

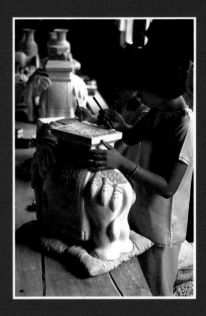

Above and Left: *Painting ceramic elephants, pottery, elephants ready for shipping at the ceramic factory in Bien Hoa.*
Left Bottom: *Working on an irrigation ditch near Long Hai.*

Facing Page: *Farm scene in Dong Nai province.*

Right: Water buffalo and a wagon near Long Hai.
Below: Buddhist Monks in Dong Nai province.

Facing Page: A wedding scene in Long Hai.

Right: Fisherman are among the very few people who occupy the areas along the beaches of Long Hai.
Below: A former French villa is being restored to serve as a hotel at Long Hai.

Left: *Fisherman coming in to the small harbor at Long Hai.*
Below: *Lotus blossoms in bloom near Long Hai.*

Above: *The Emperor's tomb west of Hue. It is not known precisely where the emperor Khai Dinh was buried, but this tomb for him was built in 1916.*
Right: *Traditional medicine practice in the market place of Nha Trang.*
FRED ROHRBACH PHOTO

Vietnam isn't quite a tourist destination yet, but it's readying to welcome travelers. With wars and struggles taking place for almost 50 years, Vietnam was hardly a hospitable place to visit. But now the leadership recognizes the importance of tourism in building an economy and is attempting to develop the industry and to make it easier for would-be visitors to see the country.

As of this writing, visas still need to be obtained in advance before permission is granted to enter Vietnam. In most nations one only needs a valid passport and entry is granted upon arrival. In the case of Vietnam, visas must be requested through a Vietnamese embassy if a country has relations with Vietnam or, in the United States, through the Vietnamese United Nations delegation in New York. U.S. citizens also may apply for a visa in another country such as Thailand. At the present, visas take approximately a month or perhaps a little less to obtain. Former Vietnamese citizens should allow four to six weeks. The government of Vietnam encourages overseas Vietnamese to return for visits to their homeland.

It's not difficult to get to Vietnam, although very few airlines include the country on their routes and flights are not on daily schedules. For individuals and group tours, the most common point of departure to Vietnam is Bangkok, Thailand, and the most usual first stop is Hanoi or Ho Chi Minh City. Thai Airways International and Hang Khong Vietnam (Air Vietnam) fly into Hanoi and Ho Chi Minh City several times a week. Air France also flies into Ho Chi Minh City from Bangkok, and Phillipine Airlines has a schedule from Manila. One can also return from Hanoi the same way, but more commonly travelers go south by plane, train or vehicle to Ho Chi Minh City and fly back to Bangkok. However, as tourism opens further, more organizations are likely to offer tours with their own arrangements and other airlines will schedule departures from more cities.

Much of the nation is inaccessible by convenient transportation. Hang Khong Vietnam flies to several of the major cities, including Hue, Da Nang, Nha Trang, Hanoi and Ho Chi Minh City, but they do not have daily flights and are heavily overbooked. A train runs between Hanoi and Ho Chi Minh City and a public bus system exists throughout the nation. However, it would be very difficult for a foreigner to travel this way. The only other means of travel for any distance in the country is by a government-rented van or vehicle accompanied by a guide and driver; this is the most reliable method.

Even if it were practical to visit most areas of the country, the time required to thoroughly see this land would be prohibitive for most people. The poor roads, especially in the north and in some areas of the central highlands, do not allow for covering much territory. In the south the highways tend to be better. Vietnam is a poor country and has higher priorities than patching roads for fast travel. The government owns the few available vehicles and the Vietnamese travel by public bus, bicycle or Honda, or they walk.

Accommodations in this southeast Asian nation are for the most part strictly Vietnamese. No western hotels exist. Ho Chi Minh City, formerly Saigon, in the south, has a few bigger semi-modern hotels, remnants of

A "taxi driver" in Bien Hoa, proud owner of the 40- to 50-year-old Citroen.

Top Left: *Eating on the street in Hanoi.*
Top Right: *Looking at the Rex Hotel in Ho Chi Minh City.*
Above: *Carrying wood for construction in Ha Nam Ninh province, northern Vietnam.*

American and other foreign presence in the country until 1975. However, beyond Ho Chi Minh City you'll notice a marked change in the quality of the accommodations compared to what westerners are accustomed to. The more isolated the area and the smaller the population, the lower the quality of guest housing. In many instances you are not assured of having water, a working fan, or air-conditioning to fend off the tropical heat. Travelers will see Vietnam for what it is, and much the way the Vietnamese see it. The country wishes to embark on a program of improving the quality of their visitor facilities but this will be a slow process. Vietnam is now adventure travel at its best.

The most practical way to visit Vietnam is not the way we did but via a tour group. It is virtually impossible at this time for an individual to get a visa to travel throughout the country. For tour groups, see your travel agency and ask them to research this for you. Although what you can see with a group will be limited, a tour will be valuable for those wanting a glimpse of Vietnam. Hopefully it will become easier for one person or a few people to obtain visas. But with no drive-it-yourself rental cars available and government restriction, that is out for now. The best bet is to design a custom tour for your group through a tour operator. With a tour group the difficulties of travel arrangements can be avoided and the costs fixed. If you receive permission to work on a project as an individual, the charges are considerable and planning destinations within a time frame can be frustrating.

How do you pay for all this? Tour groups collect up front and all major expenses are covered. For the lone journalist or researcher almost all of the hotels, government guides, fees, use of a vehicle and in-country plane fares must be paid in dollars and it's expensive. Vehicle rental runs from 25 to 60 cents a kilometer. Credit cards and travelers checks are not accepted.

You can purchase goods and food outside the hotels with the local currency called the dong. The hotels charge more for food and it is likely to be westernized.

There are several official currency rates: one at the state bank, another at local hotels, and then there's the black market trade. At this time Vietnam is experiencing extreme inflation, as high as 800 to 1,000 percent a year, so currency exchange rates change almost daily. No meaningful recommendations on exchanging money can be given here. One caution, however, is not to change money on the street when the offer is made, as the black market exchange is illegal and you may be set up for an arrest. Other things, owing to legalities, must be discovered by each individual traveler when they visit the country.

Railroad coach car off Route 1 north of Phu Ly.
FRED ROHRBACH PHOTO

SUSIE GRAETZ PHOTO

Rick Graetz is president of American Geographic Publishing, Helena, Montana, whose imprint creates a series of regional color photography and geographic books of the states. A mountain climber, explorer and professional backpacking outfitter, he is author and photographer of several outdoor books.

Fred Rohrbach, of Kent, Washington, was one of the last Americans to leave Vietnam during April 1975—and he was one of the first to return after the war. As president of his business, A-America, he lived in Vietnam for several years. He also served in the U.S. Army's 173rd Airborne Brigade in Binh Dinh province from 1968 to 1969.

Stanley Karnow has written about Vietnam since 1959 as a correspondent for Time/Life, *Saturday Evening Post*, the *Washington Post*, as special correspondent for NBC News, and foreign affairs editor of the *New Republic*. Karnow is author of *Vietnam: A History*, and was chief correspondent for the PBS series "Vietnam: A Television History."

School children on the road between
Haiphong and Ha Long Bay.